INTRODUCTION

With its long tradition of a monarchy that can be traced back to the 9th century, the UK has a wealth of royal houses, castles and palaces that are truly fascinating. Each building has a unique story that spans the centuries, told through architecture, interior decoration, precious artworks ... and indeed their gardens, which have their own tales to tell.

As kings and queens have put their individual stamps on their properties and land, reflecting the tastes and fashions of the day, we see the evolution of society and chart the progress of the royal line through the colourful personalities who have lived in these homes.

While many of the buildings have performed a formal function – and often still do – they have also been homes: the setting for births, deaths, marriages, intrigue, politics, entertainment, happiness and sorrow. Within the walls and grounds of these royal homes, the history of Britain continues to be written.

The Sunken Garden, Kensington Palace.

HAMPTON COURT PALACE

O ne of the UK's most impressive and fascinating royal homes is Hampton Court Palace, most famous as the residence of King Henry VIII and his six wives.

Built in 1515 as a home for Cardinal Thomas Wolsey, the king took possession of Hampton Court when Wolsey fell from favour having failed to secure an annulment of Henry's marriage to Catherine of Aragon.

Set in an ideal location on the banks of the River Thames, the palace provided easy access by boat to London when roads were muddy tracks. Henry enlarged the palace, paying special attention to the kitchen, fond as he was of eating and entertaining. Much of the original Tudor red-brick exterior remains, including Anne Boleyn's Gateway, with its special feature of an astronomical clock.

Following the death of Elizabeth I, Hampton Court was largely ignored by future monarchs until William III and Mary II modernised it, with Sir Christopher Wren creating both the King's Apartments and the Queen's State Apartments. After Mary's death, William lost interest in the unfinished project, and the works were finally completed under George II, the last monarch to live here.

BELOW: With its crenellated towers, red brick and heraldic animals, the Great Gatehouse is Tudor architecture at its finest. Decorative brick chimneys were the height of fashion and at Hampton Court no two are the same.

HAMPTON COURT GARDENS

The present-day gardens take their appearance from the late 17th century. The general layout is grandiose, complementing Wren's palace design; three avenues radiate from a semicircular parterre, the central avenue being in the form of a canal, the Long Water, created by Charles II in 1662.

As well as a reconstruction of William III's Privy Garden, there is a Sunken Garden, Fountain Garden, Wilderness, Magic Garden and Tiltyard, which, before becoming a kitchen garden in the 17th century, was the site for Henry VIII's jousting competitions.

Two remarkable features are the Maze, planted in hornbeam for William III, although since replaced by hedging, and the Great Vine, planted in 1728 for George II by Lancelot 'Capability' Brown. Thought to be the oldest and largest vine in the world, it is still producing fruit today.

ABOVE: The baroque Privy Garden has been reconstructed to accurately mimic its creation by William III in 1702 and the design includes the original wrought iron screens at the river end.

THE BANQUETING HOUSE, WHITEHALL

The Banqueting House is the only remaining building from the Palace of Whitehall, the main residence of English monarchs from 1530 to 1698. The Palace of Whitehall has its origins in medieval times as the London base for the Archbishops of York, when it was known as York Place. It was Cardinal Thomas Wolsey's home until, as with Hampton Court, Henry VIII laid claim to it. Henry turned it into a magnificent palace and changed its name to Whitehall.

In 1619, Inigo Jones was commissioned by James I to build a grand entertainment venue next to Whitehall Palace. The Banqueting House was a spectacular achievement, further enhanced in 1636, under Charles I, with ceiling paintings by the Flemish artist Rubens, each glorifying the Stuart monarchy. Ironically, when he commissioned the work, Charles was not to know that the Banqueting House would be the location of his execution in 1649.

The building's original façade was replaced in both 1774 and 1829 with the Portland stone that gives it the grey-white appearance it has today.

QUEEN'S HOUSE, GREENWICH

Standing on the banks of the Thames at Greenwich, over which it has panoramic views, the Queen's House is one of the finest buildings from the Stuart period and the first in England created in the pure classical Palladian style.

When James VI of Scotland became James I of England in 1603, he moved his household to London and the Palace of Placentia at Greenwich, birthplace of both Henry VIII and Elizabeth I. Built on the site of the former gatehouse of Placentia Palace by the architect Inigo Jones, the Queen's House, or Manor of Greenwich as it was then, was a gift from James I to his wife Anne of Denmark, reputedly as an apology for swearing at her when she accidentally killed one of his dogs while hunting. On receipt of her gift, Anne commissioned Jones to build a new house but the innovative project came to a halt in 1618 when Anne became ill and subsequently died. It was not until 1629 that work on the house was restarted by Charles I, who gave the house to his French wife, Henrietta Maria.

BELOW: **The original main house, built between 1616 and 1635, is linked by colonnades to wings added in the early 19th century.**

CIVIL WAR, THE RESTORATION AND BEYOND

Work was completed in 1636 and Henrietta Maria enjoyed the house until 1642 when civil war broke out. With her husband executed by Cromwell's Roundheads, the house and its contents were seized by the State, while Henrietta Maria fled to France, returning to Greenwich in 1660 with the Restoration of the monarchy. The new 'Merry Monarch' Charles II spent extravagantly on refurbishments.

The house remained a royal residence until 1805 when George III gave it to the Royal Naval Asylum, a charity that provided an education for the orphans of seamen. It was run under the auspices of the Royal Hospital School, with two wings added to accommodate children and staff. In 1934 the house came into the ownership of the National Maritime Museum and in the late 20th century the building was restored, with parts resembling its former appearance in the late 17th century.

OPULENT CEILING PANELS

Prominent European artists were commissioned to paint ceiling panels at the Queen's House, since replaced with modern copies. The originals are in London's Marlborough House.

INIGO JONES' MASTERPIECE

In its day, the brilliant white house with its glorious H-shaped symmetry, elegant columns and perfect proportions was considered radical in its design. Ironically, its modernity had its roots in the ancient Roman world, Jones having travelled extensively in Italy where he became fascinated by the work of Palladio. The Queen's House was his first venture based on his interpretation of the Italian classical style.

Both James I and Charles I were lavish spenders, allowing Jones to create an interior as extravagant as the exterior. At its heart is the Great Hall, rising through two storeys to form a cube, with a black-and-white marble floor and a colour scheme of gold and white. Leading off the hall is one of Jones' most beautiful creations: the Tulip Staircase, the earliest unsupported central spiral staircase in England.

ABOVE: The helical Tulip Staircase with its lantern above was considered an engineering marvel at the time of its construction.

OSBORNE HOUSE

Osborne House on the Isle of Wight became a royal residence when it was purchased by Queen Victoria and her consort Prince Albert in 1845. Victoria held the island in special affection as she had holidayed there as a girl with her mother, while its outlook reminded Albert of one of his favourite places, the Bay of Naples.

Victoria and Albert created a residence suited to their taste – and with space for their nine children – by building a new house in the Italian Renaissance style. The majority of the work was finished by 1851, with final completion in 1891.

The ground floor is formal and features the ornate Durbar Room, created in the style of the British Raj, with many artworks from the Indian subcontinent. In contrast, the first floor was created as a homely environment for the royal children. Osborne House remained Queen Victoria's favourite residence and she visited frequently, even after Albert's death.

ALBERT'S INFLUENCE

Both the house and gardens were a joy to the royal couple, with Albert given a free rein with the landscaping as this was a private residence, rather than one owned by the Crown. The descendant of a myrtle plant brought over from Germany still provides sprigs of the shrub for royal wedding bouquets to this day, a tradition started on the marriage of Victoria and Albert's eldest daughter to German Emperor Frederick III.

PRESENTED TO THE NATION

Following Victoria's death in 1901, Edward VII presented it to the nation on his Coronation in 1902. At different times it became a training site for the Royal Naval College and the King Edward VII Retirement Home for Officers, but today Osborne House is cared for by English Heritage and is a major tourist attraction.

ROYAL PAVILION, BRIGHTON

The Royal Pavilion's history is rooted in the 1780s, when George, Prince of Wales, later George IV, rented a lodging house in the seaside resort of Brighton to allow him to 'take the waters'. He later purchased the lodging house and commissioned architect Henry Holland to redesign it as a seaside home, named Marine Pavilion.

George soon found the house too cramped for the lavish entertaining he so enjoyed and, on his appointment as Prince Regent in 1811, he set about transforming the Pavilion into a fantasy palace. Leading architect John Nash was put in charge of the works, based on the oriental designs fashionable at the time. No expense was spared on features that today have been meticulously recreated.

When Queen Victoria inherited the building, she found it out of keeping with her sensibilities so sold it to the town. It became a popular tourist attraction and was restored in the following decades. Efforts to recreate the Regency style of the Pavilion commenced after the Second World War and work continues to ensure this building, with its iconic domes, enchants visitors with its exotic design and stunning interiors.

ABOVE: With the assistance of London builder and architect Thomas Cubitt, the reconstructed Osborne House was designed by Prince Albert himself in the Italian Renaissance style, complete with two dramatic belvedere towers.

WINDSOR CASTLE

D ating from the time of William the Conqueror, the castle has a 900-year association with the Royal Family and, indeed, the surname Windsor was adopted by George V in 1917 in reference to this heritage, thereby creating the House of Windsor.

Today Windsor Castle is both a working building and a royal home, to which visiting Heads of State are welcomed and where official ceremonies, such as the investiture of Knights of the Garter, are held.

The first time a royal building was erected on the site was after the Norman Conquest in 1066, when William I built a series of motte and bailey defences around London. Sitting above the River Thames, and approximately 20 miles (32km) from London, a mostly wooden castle was built to protect the western approach to the capital.

RIGHT: St George's Chapel is considered to be among the finest examples of Gothic architecture in England.

BELOW: Two hundred steps lead to the top of Windsor Castle's iconic Round Tower, from where it is possible to enjoy panoramic views towards the London skyline.

A ROYAL RESIDENCE

Windsor Castle became a royal residence in the 12th century under Henry I and it has continued as such ever since. It is the longest-occupied palace in Europe as well as the largest occupied castle in the world.

As wood made way for stone, the castle fortifications became stronger and, before Henry III built a luxurious palace within the keep, the castle had survived a prolonged siege during the First Barons' War of 1215–17.

Over the centuries the castle underwent many changes as successive sovereigns introduced their individual tastes to the building. The first to do so to any notable extent was Edward III, who was born in the castle. In the 1360s, he created a palace which included the impressive St George's Hall for use of the Knights of the Garter, a chivalric order he founded.

Around 150 years later, Henry VIII made substantial alterations when he built the North Wharf terrace. Elizabeth I used the fortified castle as a safe haven when necessary, while James I, in the 17th century, enjoyed hunting in the surrounding forests. By this point, Windsor Castle had become an important royal court away from the bustle of London.

ENGLISH CIVIL WAR

During the English Civil War of 1642–51, the castle became headquarters for the Parliamentarians and a prison for Charles I prior to his beheading in London in 1649, his body then returned to Windsor for burial in St George's Chapel. Throughout this troubled period, the castle fell into disrepair and its contents were looted. In 1653, when Oliver Cromwell was made Lord Protector, the building became one of his official residences.

The new Commonwealth established by the puritan republican Cromwell in 1649 was short-lived and two years after his death in 1658, the monarchy was restored.

THE RESTORATION AND BEYOND

Charles II was duly declared the lawful ruler of England, and the country's social pendulum swung towards more liberal attitudes, including a revived appreciation of the arts. Charles modernised Windsor Castle, and many of the features seen today date from his reign.

George I disliked the castle and it fell to George III and George IV in the 18th and 19th centuries to instigate major changes that included introducing the French Rococo style and increasing the height of the famous Round Tower. In 1845, Queen Victoria, who made the castle her main residence, initiated the opening of the State Apartments for public viewing.

A longer period of development occurred under Edward VII, with redecoration and decluttering top of the agenda, a process continued by George V, whose watchword for the castle was that everything had to be 'of the best'.

MORE MODERN TIMES

Windsor Castle was to become the preferred home of George VI, Queen Elizabeth II's father, and his family. Having spent much of her young life there, it has a special place in The Queen's heart and she was visibly upset when part of the building was destroyed by fire in 1992. Since then, the damage has been sensitively restored.

Today, Windsor Castle is where The Queen spends most weekends and hosts many official functions. In addition to the castle being a working palace, it is also a major tourist attraction, with the Changing of the Guard ceremony always popular with visitors. Tourists and locals alike delight in seeing the Guards marching with their band from their barracks in the town to the castle via the High Street.

RIGHT: The Long Walk viewed from the Snow Hill end, where is sited the mounted King George III statue – known as the Copper Horse. The avenue was created by Charles II in an attempt to recreate the flamboyance of Versailles.

BELOW: The Changing the Guard ceremony takes place within the Castle walls in the Quadrangle if The Queen is in residence and in the Lower Ward if she is not.

THE GREAT PARK

The Crown Estate at Windsor is comprised of the landscaped Great Park covering 5,000 acres (2,020 hectares). The Grade I listed park, open to the public free of charge, is characterised by its ancient oaks and has a deer park, woodland, ponds and lawns, as well as the Long Walk, a 3-mile (5-km) track, which provides a traffic-free haven in the town. Created by Charles II, it runs from Snow Hill – with its wonderful view towards London – to the castle.

Originally lined with elm trees, the Long Walk now features oak, horse chestnut and London planes, which form a spectacular wide avenue. The estate generally is actively involved in conservation, to include the propagation of a further 9,000 trees from its ancient oaks to preserve genetic continuity.

The Great Park is also home to several houses, including the Royal Lodge, Cumberland Lodge and Fort Belvedere.

FROGMORE

In the Home Park, the private grounds next to Windsor Castle, is the Grade I listed neoclassical Frogmore House, which dates from 1680. The house has had several royal residents since Queen Charlotte, wife of George III, who acquired it in 1792. Queen Victoria and Prince Albert are both buried in the Royal Mausoleum here. Today Frogmore House is used for entertaining and was the venue for the wedding reception of the Duke and Duchess of Sussex in 2018 following their marriage in St George's Chapel within the castle walls. The couple moved from Kensington Palace into Frogmore Cottage, a Grade II listed property that previously housed estate workers. Extensive renovations and alterations were carried out and, due to the fact it is situated just yards from the Long Walk, ultra-tight security systems were installed.

ST JAMES'S PALACE

A hospital for lepers might seem an unlikely location for the creation of a palace, but the site upon which St James's Palace now stands was exactly that. Previously the Hospital of St James, it was acquired by Henry VIII in 1531 who built this royal home to form part of the Palace of Westminster. Tudor architecture is particularly evident in the crenellated gatehouse, decorated with an H for Henry and an A for his second wife, Anne Boleyn.

In 1649, St James's was where Charles I spent his final night before his execution at Whitehall, after which Oliver Cromwell turned the palace into barracks for his Parliamentarian troops. After the Restoration, Charles II reclaimed the palace and laid out the adjacent St James's Park, while James II commissioned Christopher Wren to add magnificent State Rooms. St James's became the principal royal London residence following the loss in 1698 of Whitehall Palace in a fire, and it remained as such for George I and George II.

FORMAL FUNCTIONALITY

George III, however, disliked the palace's maze of Tudor corridors. He purchased Buckingham House – Buckingham Palace's predecessor – and used St James's mainly for formal occasions. From the reign of Queen Victoria, the palace functioned mainly as an administrative centre and so it remains today. Although no longer a residence for the monarch, some members of the Royal Family still live here, and its sumptuous Throne Room is where the Lord Mayor usually presents an address of welcome to visiting heads of state.

CLARENCE HOUSE

In contrast to its neighbour St James's Palace, to which it is attached, Clarence House is a typical late-Georgian mansion house with all the hallmarks of its creator, John Nash, and typifies buildings of that era.

The house, built between 1825 and 1827, was commissioned by the Duke of Clarence, later William IV. William disliked St James's Palace and made the spacious Clarence House his main residence. He was, however, the only reigning monarch ever to live here; Buckingham Palace became the preferred main royal home and Clarence House was relegated in importance.

Clarence House has been home to several senior members of the Royal Family since the mid-20th century, including Princess Elizabeth and her husband the Duke of Edinburgh who lived here prior to her accession to the throne. After Queen Elizabeth II's coronation in 1953, the newly widowed Queen Mother moved in and lived here until her death in 2002. The following year, Prince Charles made Clarence House his official London residence; he instigated changes to modernise the interior while retaining its historic character.

Today, as well being the London home of Prince Charles and the Duchess of Cornwall, Clarence House is used for official receptions and entertaining, with parts of the house and gardens opened to the public each August.

BOMBED IN THE BLITZ

Clarence House was badly damaged during the Second World War and though today little of Nash's original work remains, the building has been sensitively restored to its former glory.

LEFT: The Tudor northern gatehouse of St James's Palace bears a clock dated 1731 from the reign of George II. To the right is the Chapel Royal, where it is said Mary I's heart is buried beneath the choir stalls.

RIGHT: Prince Charles's London home, Clarence House, contains new artworks from the Royal Collection as well as pieces owned personally by the Prince.

KENSINGTON PALACE

S et in Kensington Gardens, this Jacobean palace, in the heart of the Royal Borough of Kensington and Chelsea, has been a royal home since the late 17th century. It was built in 1605 by Sir George Coppin when Kensington was a rural village surrounded by open fields. William III and Mary II were its first royal residents; William was afflicted with chronic asthma and it was thought that the countryside location would alleviate the symptoms, and Kensington Palace – or Nottingham House as it was then called – seemed ideal as a country retreat.

Like most royal homeowners, William and Mary altered and expanded the building, commissioning Christopher Wren to carry out the work, and they moved in just before Christmas 1689. After their deaths, Queen Anne continued the work they had started. She created the Queen's Apartments, complete with a specially designed staircase to allow her to descend gracefully in long, full-skirted gowns.

George I spent lavishly, creating three new State Rooms and, in 1722, commissioning William Kent to decorate the walls and ceilings with dramatic trompe l'oeil designs. His son George II was the last reigning monarch to use the palace as a home but took little interest in the house, allowing it to fall into disrepair following the death of his wife, Queen Caroline.

From the 1760s, less senior royals lived at Kensington Palace – although Princess Victoria, later Queen Victoria, was born here – as Buckingham Palace became the favoured home for reigning sovereigns.

Like Clarence House, Kensington Palace suffered bomb damage in the Second World War and it was some years before it was habitable once more, although since that time, many residents, including The Queen's sister Princess Margaret who lived here following her marriage, have added their personality to the apartments, by redecorating and carrying out alterations.

HOME TO SENIOR ROYALS

In 1981 the newly married Prince of Wales and Princess Diana moved in, and Princes William and Harry spent a large part of their childhoods here. After being divorced from her husband, Diana continued to live here until her death in 1997, and it was from the palace that her coffin left for her funeral at Westminster Abbey.

In 2011, Prince William and his wife, the Duchess of Cambridge, moved from the two-bedroomed Nottingham Cottage, a small house within Kensington Palace's grounds, into the four-storey apartment formerly occupied by Princess Margaret.

Prior to their move to Frogmore Cottage in Windsor, Nottingham Cottage was home to Prince Harry and his wife, the Duchess of Sussex, while Harry's cousin Princess Eugenie moved into the three-bedroom Ivy Cottage within the palace grounds following her marriage to Jack Brooksbank in 2018.

FABULOUS EXHIBITIONS

Following a two-year renovation programme commenced in 2010, the State Rooms offer visitors the latest digital interactive displays among the many varied exhibits to be seen.

ABOVE: The King's Staircase painted by William Kent displays a trompe l'oeil depiction of George I's court.

OPPOSITE: Sir Christopher Wren reorientated the house to face west and laid out the gardens in the formal Dutch style.

KENSINGTON GARDENS

Adjoining Hyde Park to the east with the Serpentine lake at the boundary, Kensington Gardens now form one of the Royal Parks of London and cover 242 acres (98 hectares).

Surrounding Kensington Palace, the gardens were once set in a rural environment but today, bordered by the central London boroughs of Bayswater, Kensington and Chelsea, and Knightsbridge, they provide a welcome green space in the urban landscape.

In the reign of Henry VIII, the gardens were part of Hyde Park and used for deer hunting.

It wasn't until William III and his wife Queen Mary II took over the palace that the land around the house was separated to form what would be recognised as gardens. To reflect William's Dutch heritage, the new gardens, with formal flowerbeds and box hedges, were laid out in the style of those of his homeland.

On the accession of Queen Anne in 1702, the gardens took on a more English appearance, and Anne also created The Orangery – a grand conservatory – to house the citrus trees of which she was so fond, and to provide a venue for entertaining.

A PUBLIC PARK

It was Queen Caroline, wife of George II, who created the park in the style that we see today, commencing the work in 1728, and adding the water features – the Serpentine lake, Round Pond and Long Water. However, throughout the 18th century, and despite their size and space, the gardens were only open to the public on Saturdays, and then only if the visitors were 'respectably dressed'. This may have been a way of preventing them from acquiring a dubious reputation as pleasure gardens, such as those at Vauxhall Gardens on the south bank of the River Thames, which had attracted a very mixed class of visitors.

THE WHITE GARDEN

Aside from the formal gardens, what was known as the Sunken Garden was created in 1908 on what had been an untidy area occupied by sheds. The design of this section of the gardens harks back to the 18th century, with paving, formal flowerbeds and an ornamental pond with a fountain that was created from an 18th-century cistern that had once been inside the palace. Bordering this garden is Cradle Walk, a beautiful arched arbour created from coppiced lime that provides a tunnel effect but with viewpoints at intervals from which the garden can be enjoyed.

Seasonal planting had always ensured the Sunken Garden was a riot of colour, but in 2018 it underwent a transformation. Gone were the colours and in their place white blooms, along with a new name, the White Garden. Planted to commemorate the 20th anniversary of the death of Princess Diana, who was fond of the Sunken Garden, today its chic and simple elegance makes it a place of quiet contemplation.

OPPOSITE: Kensington Palace and its gardens adjoining Hyde Park provide a green oasis within central London.

BELOW: The replanted Sunken Garden was renamed the White Garden in memory of Princess Diana.

MEGHAN'S WEDDING BOUQUET

Flowers from the White Garden were used in the wedding bouquet of Meghan Markle and picked personally by her groom, Prince Harry.

KEW PALACE

Kew Palace was a royal home for 90 years, from 1728 until 1818. The smallest of the palaces, it was built in 1631 by Flemish merchant Samuel Fortrey on the site of an existing house.

The Flemish influence is evident in its architecture; then known as the Dutch House, it was leased to George II and Queen Caroline in 1728. Opposite was Kew House, leased in 1730 to their son Frederick; it was renamed the White House after Frederick had turned it into a grand home with a white stucco exterior.

From 1772, George III and his wife initially used the White House as a country residence, while their sons George and Frederick moved into the Dutch House, purchased by the Royal Family in 1781.

BELOW: The stepped gables of Kew Palace led to the house being known as the Dutch House despite this being a Flemish design.

THE MADNESS OF KING GEORGE

As George III became increasingly ill (recent research suggests with bipolar disorder), he and Queen Charlotte moved to live full time in the White House, away from busy London, and they planned to build an extravagant palace on the adjacent site. However, by 1801 the king's 'madness' meant he felt a prisoner in the house, so he moved to Windsor Castle and ultimately had the White House demolished. Today only a sundial marks where it once stood.

After both George and Charlotte died, the Dutch House was closed and its demolition planned. Fortunately, George IV had a change of heart and it then became known as Kew Palace.

Later monarchs showed no desire to live in the house. In Victoria's reign it was transferred to the ownership of Kew Gardens and was opened to the public for the first time in 1899 – and remains so today, under the care of Historic Royal Palaces.

ROYAL BOTANIC GARDENS, KEW

The current botanic gardens (now a UNESCO World Heritage Site) were founded as a national resource in 1840 and today cover an enormous 330 acres (133 hectares) with more than 30,000 varieties of living plants.

It was in the 18th century that the original, smaller, garden was first laid out by Queen Caroline, wife of George II. Subsequently, the planting of the eastern section surrounding the White House was commissioned by Caroline's daughter-in-law, Augusta, the Dowager Princess of Wales.

The world was gradually opening up through exploration; many exotic species were being discovered, and it was Princess Augusta's aim to create a 'botanick garden'. The Great Pagoda, a gift to her in 1762, remains one of Kew's most famous landmarks.

In 1772, the gardens of the royal estates of Kew and Richmond were joined and further extended in stages in the 19th century until the grounds reached their current size.

FAMOUS GLASSHOUSES

The expansion enabled more plants to be grown, plus buildings and glasshouses to be erected, including the Palm House; built 1844–48, it represents the first large-scale use of wrought iron in a structure.

The neoclassical Nash Conservatory, designed by architect John Nash, was moved from Buckingham Palace to Kew by William IV in 1836. The climatically controlled Princess of Wales Conservatory was opened in 1987, and houses orchids, lilies, carnivorous plants and bromeliads. During its construction, a time capsule containing seeds of crops and endangered species was buried on the site.

ABOVE: The Palm House with its hand-blown glass and extensive wrought iron was a marvel of the Victorian age; today it houses exotic plants of the rainforest.

KEW GARDENS TODAY

The collection today includes thousands of species of plants from across the world, from all climates and terrain. With a wide range of exhibits and activities, there is something to delight every visitor, not least the Treetop Walkway which provides views over the gardens and beyond.

BUCKINGHAM PALACE

An iconic building that is instantly recognisable, Buckingham Palace is the most important of the royal residences and has been the official London home of British sovereigns since 1837. In 1705, a large villa called Buckingham House was erected as a commission for John Sheffield, Duke of Buckingham, but it was not until 1762 that it fell into royal hands when it was purchased for £28,000 by King George III for his wife, Queen Charlotte, and renamed the Queen's House. At that time, in stark contrast to today, the surrounding area was rural, and the house offered the tranquillity of a pastoral life.

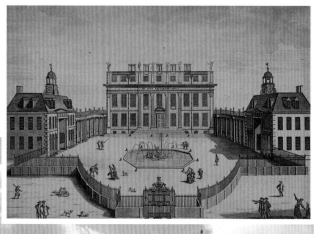

LEFT: The original façade of what was then the country manor known as Buckingham House, built in 1705.

BELOW: Buckingham Palace has greatly expanded over the centuries and the original soft stone of the façade has been replaced with harder Portland stone.

FROM HOUSE TO PALACE

It was George III's successor, George IV, who began to turn the house into the palace that we know today. On his accession in 1820, initially he did not intend to live in the house – but he changed his mind and in 1826 commissioned leading architect John Nash to turn the house into a palace fit for a king, with a massive budget of £450,000.

The house was doubled in size and the façade, typical of Nash's style, was French neoclassical, in soft-hued Bath stone. The north and south wings of the house were demolished and rebuilt on a grand scale, to include a courtyard with a huge triumphal arch, known as the Marble Arch. Although by now Nash was over budget, new State Rooms were built leading from the Picture Gallery, and one of the palace's most elaborate features was created, the Grand Staircase leading from the Grand Hall.

In 1830, without seeing his vision for the palace come to fruition, George died and his successor, his younger brother William IV, in an attempt to contain the spiralling costs, sacked Nash and hired Edward Blore to finish the work. Unfortunately, like his older brother, William was never to live in the palace, and it was Queen Victoria who became the first monarch to use it as an official London residence when she became queen in 1837. She was also the first British sovereign to leave for her Coronation from Buckingham Palace, as the building was now called.

the front of the palace, the work being finally completed in 1914, just before the outbreak of the First World War.

THE PALACE TODAY

Although Queen Elizabeth II has an apartment here, today it is very much a working palace, where official duties are carried out, including investitures and the conferring of knighthoods. Foreign dignitaries and other VIPs are entertained at State banquets, and large events, such as The Queen's Diamond Jubilee celebrations and royal wedding receptions, are based at the palace. One of the most important events of the annual calendar is a reception for members of the diplomatic corps, which takes place in November and uses all the State Rooms. Buckingham Palace is also the location of The Queen's weekly audiences with her Prime Minister.

FINE PUBLIC VIEWING

Buckingham Palace is home to many valuable works of art and many are on display for visitors to enjoy. These include not only numerous paintings, in particular works by Rubens, Van Dyck, Stubbs and Canaletto, but also

VICTORIAN EXPANSION

Queen Victoria had her own thoughts about Buckingham Palace and, still with Blore in charge, set about further expansion to provide nurseries and more guest bedrooms. A fourth wing was created, for which it was necessary to relocate the Marble Arch, which now stands at the north-east corner of Hyde Park. Funding for the extensive work was largely raised from the sale of the Royal Pavilion at Brighton.

Blore had favoured soft French stone but by 1913, in the reign of George V, the decision was made to replace this facing with harder Portland stone, as the former was suffering deterioration as a result of the polluting sooty atmosphere of the time. The huge task was carried out under the guidance of architect Sir Aston Webb.

George V also saw the completion of the gates and railings leading into the forecourt at

sculptures, furniture, porcelain, furnishings and photographs. These can be seen in the State Rooms and The Queen's Gallery, which are open to the public, often with specific themed exhibitions on display. Visitors can also view the Throne Room and the Ballroom, and marvel at the sweeping Grand Staircase, its low, wide stairs allowing for dramatic, entrances and exits, while its portrait-adorned walls exude a sense of history.

OPPOSITE: **The bronze Grand Staircase was designed by John Nash and is illuminated by a glass dome above.**

RIGHT: **The Palace Ballroom is transformed for a State Banquet featuring George IV's silver gilt Grand Service.**

FAMOUS BALCONY

It is perhaps the balcony for which Buckingham Palace is most famous. Having commissioned the palace wing featuring the balcony to mark the opening of the Great Exhibition in 1851, Queen Victoria was the first monarch to appear upon it before her subjects. Since then, it has been the traditional spot for members of the Royal Family to gather before the general public on important occasions, in particular weddings and the annual Trooping the Colour ceremony, as well as one-off events, such as VE Day in 1945, the Queen Mother's 100th birthday in 2000 and The Queen's Diamond Jubilee in 2012. It has also become the location for the 'balcony kiss' at royal weddings taking place in London, a tradition started by Prince Charles when he married Lady Diana Spencer in 1981.

BUCKINGHAM PALACE GARDENS

The gardens of Buckingham Palace represent a magnificent green space within the City of Westminster, stretching as they do to 42 acres (17 hectares).

GRAND GARDEN DESIGNS

The original gardens were landscaped in the 18th century by the great British garden designer Lancelot 'Capability' Brown. His landscapes were intended to appear natural but, in fact, everything was meticulously planned to be balanced, elegant and coherent, with visual surprises and illusions certain to delight. With such a noble heritage, it is perhaps surprising that George IV, when he embarked on the rebuilding of Buckingham House, chose to commission a redesign of the gardens by William Townsend Alton.

SPECIAL FEATURES

Today, the gardens feature a wide variety of plants, especially trees, many of them exotic, which can be viewed via gravel walkways. Points of special interest are a mulberry tree from the reign of James I and a lake created in 1828, at which time it was home to a flock of flamingos.

Works of art in the form of statues abound, the most notable being the Waterloo Vase, a 15-foot (4.6-metre) urn made of Carrara marble, said to have been commissioned by Napoleon at the turn of the 19th century in anticipation of his victories in what became the Napoleonic Wars. Following his defeat, the roughly hewn urn was presented to George IV – at that time Prince Regent – who intended to install the piece at Windsor Castle. Unfortunately, the urn was so heavy, at 15 tons, it was feared that the floor would not support it and it was, instead, given to the National Gallery, where it was kept until it was re-presented to Edward VII in 1906. He placed the huge piece in the Buckingham Palace gardens, where it has remained ever since.

GARDEN PARTIES

The gardens are generally not accessible to the public except during August and September when the palace is open and visitors have access to a section of the grounds. However, every year around 30,000 people have the chance to see the gardens at three special events held during May and June, when The Queen hosts her famous garden parties, a tradition originally started by Queen Victoria. Guests from all walks of life are invited in special recognition of specific achievements or as reward for public service. The Queen, Duke of Edinburgh and other members of the Royal Family mingle with guests as they enjoy afternoon tea in this green oasis in the heart of London.

In addition, The Queen also gives permission for special garden parties, such as the one held annually for the Not Forgotten Association – a

LEFT: The classically designed Waterloo Vase is fashioned from a single piece of Carrara marble.

charity for wounded or sick ex-service personnel – and the party in 2018 to mark Prince Charles' 70th birthday and the charities he supports.

BELOW: The Palace gardens contain hundreds of trees which can be viewed from two and half miles of gravel walkways running throughout.

RIGHT: The Queen enjoys mingling with guests at her annual garden parties.

HIGHGROVE HOUSE AND GARDENS

Situated in rural Gloucestershire, near Tetbury, Highgrove House is the country residence of Prince Charles and his wife, Camilla, Duchess of Cornwall. A few miles away is Gatcombe Park, the country home of Charles' sister, Anne, the Princess Royal.

Highgrove is relatively modern in terms of royal homes, built 1796–98 for the Paul family. Over the centuries, various owners of the house made alterations, particularly after a major fire in 1893. In 1965 it became the home of Maurice Macmillan, son of former UK Prime Minister Harold Macmillan, and in 1980 it was bought by the Duchy of Cornwall for Prince Charles who

ABOVE: **Prince Charles remodelled Highgrove House to include a new balustrade, pediment and classical pilasters in the neoclassical Georgian style.**

wanted a home accessible from both London and Cornwall. Highgrove was deemed the ideal country retreat following his marriage to Princess Diana in 1981, and this is where their sons William and Harry spent much time as they grew up.

The three-storey Grade II listed house was originally built in the Georgian style, but in the 1980s Prince Charles remodelled it, adding neoclassical features. With his interest in the environment and sustainability, over the years His Royal Highness has added up-to-date technology in order to minimise the building's carbon footprint, such as hot-water systems powered by ground- and air-source heat pumps and biomass boilers. The house also has a sewage system that treats waste via a natural filtration method using reed beds.

HIGHGROVE GARDENS

When Prince Charles took on the house, the gardens and surrounding land had been neglected. However, following decades of hard work by him, in conjunction with gardeners and landscapers, including Miriam Rothschild and Lady Salisbury, the gardens are now a remarkable place of natural beauty, a haven for flora and fauna.

The gardens – open to the public for guided tours during certain months – are a series of interconnecting tableaux that reflect the prince's interests and include a Wildflower Meadow, Cottage Garden, Kitchen Garden and Carpet Garden. He has also encouraged the growth of rare plants and trees, some now part of the National Plant Collections.

Also within the gardens is an eclectic collection of busts of people admired by the prince, including poet Kathleen Raine, activist

Vandana Shiva, composer John Tavener and the Bishop of London Richard Chartres.

ORGANIC PRODUCE

The estate beyond the gardens comprises the organic Duchy Home Farm, where rare breed animals are raised. Prince Charles' aim has been to create a biologically sustainable farm that supports environmental and ecological conservation. Much of the food produced is sold under the Duchy Organic brand, which includes everything from biscuits to meat, from milk to ale; in 2017 it became the UK's largest organic private label brand.

BELOW: **The Highgrove shop sells organic produce grown on the Duchy Home Farm.**

FEATURES WITH A TWIST

Many features in the gardens are similar to those found in more formal settings, but at Highgrove they have a twist, with natural materials abounding. For example, close to the house is a dramatic oak pavilion created over the base of a 200-year-old Cedar of Lebanon that, due to disease, was felled in 2007.

SANDRINGHAM HOUSE

Sandringham is a manor house and estate owned by the Royal Family personally, purchased in 1862 by the future Edward VII. Set in the Norfolk countryside, Sandringham has been a favourite royal residence ever since.

The majority of the current building was erected in the 19th century, replacing earlier Elizabethan and Georgian houses. In 1863, newlyweds Prince Edward and Princess Alexandra moved in. Soon the house proved too small for their growing family and love of entertaining, and A.J. Humbert was commissioned for what was effectively a total rebuild. Fire destroyed many rooms while the house was being prepared for the prince's 50th birthday celebrations, but repairs remained faithful to Humbert's design relating to the brickwork and his use of Ketton stone.

THE GROUNDS

Edward and Alexandra transformed the gardens and wider estate, and constructed several buildings, including staff cottages, a school and a staff clubhouse. In the 1870s, a lake was drained, filled and planted with formal parterres, and, in 1912, a summerhouse – The Nest – was built. Edward VII opened the gardens to the public in 1908.

FUTURE GENERATIONS

Edward and Alexandra had transformed the gardens and wider estate. When Sandringham House passed to George V, the new king and queen were unable to move in as his father's will stipulated that Queen Alexandra had lifetime occupancy of the house. It was not until her death in 1925 that George and Mary took up residency, even though the conservative George had been perfectly content to live in York Cottage on the estate. It was from Sandringham

in 1932 that George V broadcast the first royal Christmas message, a traditional feature of that season ever since.

Like his father, George VI loved Sandringham: 'I have always been so happy here'. However, during the Second World War, economies had to be made, so the house was shut up and the family stayed in smaller properties when visiting, with the Christmas celebrations also temporarily suspended until 1945.

Having been born in York Cottage, it was in Sandringham House that the king died on 6 February 1952, aged 56. Queen Elizabeth II has traditionally spent the anniversary of her father's death and her accession to the throne

RIGHT: Sandringham's design suggests it is Jacobean but most of it was built in the 19th century, 200 years later.

SANDRINGHAM TIME

Edward VII was a keen sportsman and the estate saw elaborate weekend game shooting parties. The king even introduced 'Sandringham time', setting all clocks half an hour ahead of GMT to give extra daylight time for sport (a practice also observed at Windsor and Balmoral). This continued during George V's reign until it was abolished by Edward VIII in 1936 on the death of his father.

here, and has followed the custom established by her great-grandfather, Edward VII, of the Royal Family spending Christmas at Sandringham, and attending Sandringham church St Mary Magdalene on Christmas Day morning.

The Queen opened Sandringham House to the public on her Silver Jubilee, 1977. At certain times of year visitors can see the house, gardens and a museum in the former coach house that includes a collection of royal memorabilia charting the estate's history.

Also on the estate is Park House, birthplace of Princess Diana when her father was its tenant. Another home is Anmer Hall, the country residence of Prince William and his family.

RIGHT: The Nest summerhouse, built for Queen Alexandra in 1913, sits above the Upper Lake.

BALMORAL

Like Sandringham, Balmoral Castle does not form part of the Crown Estate, and is The Queen's private holiday residence.

Set in Aberdeenshire, the original house was a 15th-century square tower with battlements, altered most notably in 1830 when Scottish baronial-style extensions were added. Victoria and Albert, having fallen in love with the Highlands, leased the house without even seeing it, later purchasing it in 1852. To accommodate their growing family, Albert, working with the Aberdeen architect William Smith, designed a castle that some say reflects his German heritage. Albert established new plantations and buildings, including an iron bridge, designed by Isambard Kingdom Brunel, across the River Dee, increasing accessibility to the castle.

Victoria and Albert enjoyed the rural life amongst the mountains, a contrast to the time they spent in London.

AFTER VICTORIA

Despite being bereft after Albert's death, Victoria continued to visit her beloved Balmoral as often as possible. Changes by her grandson George V included the installation of electricity powered by a generator and turbine. His granddaughters, Princess Elizabeth and Princess Margaret, spent some months here during the war years, away from London, riding on the hills relatively free from supervision.

Queen Elizabeth II loves Balmoral and spends every summer here. Similarly, Prince Charles holds it in special affection.

Today the 50,000-acre (20,000-hectare) estate has four areas reserved for the protected conservation of flora and fauna.

BELOW: **The baronial-style Balmoral was built from the grey granite found on the castle's estates.**

PALACE OF HOLYROODHOUSE

Just as Buckingham Palace is The Queen's main official residence in London, the Palace of Holyroodhouse is the Scottish equivalent in Edinburgh.

Originally an Augustinian abbey founded by King David I of Scotland in 1128, the name Holyrood may be derived from him seeing a vision of the holy cross, or rood.

In the 12th century Holyrood became a royal guest house for the abbey until, in 1501, James IV built a palace adjacent to it. James V also lived here, as did his daughter, Mary Queen of Scots, who married two of her husbands within Holyrood's walls.

Work continued on the palace under James I of England (James VI of Scotland) and later Charles II, who initiated the building of the south-west tower and decorated the State Apartments sumptuously. By 1679 the palace was much as we see it today.

The Jacobite uprising in 1745 saw the Scots try to claim the British throne, but after their defeat at the Battle of Culloden in 1746, and with no Scottish monarchy, the palace lay deserted until George IV returned in 1822.

HOLYROOD IN THE TWENTIETH CENTURY

In 1911, George V and Queen Mary installed bathrooms, electricity and central heating. After extensive renovations, Holyrood was formally designated a royal residence in the 1920s, since which time it has been the grand setting for investitures, audiences and garden parties held annually by The Queen. Both the palace and grounds are open to the public.

BELOW: **The beautifully symmetrical Holyroodhouse has been a royal residence for more than 500 years.**

PLACES TO VISIT

In addition to the royal homes and gardens featured in this book, most of which are open to the public, listed here are just some of the additional places in the UK with royal links, past or present, that are well worth a visit. Please refer to their websites for details of opening days and times.

LONDON

Banqueting House, Whitehall
www.hrp.org.uk/banqueting-house

Buckingham Palace & Gardens
www.rct.uk/visit/the-state-rooms-buckingham-palace

Clarence House
www.rct.uk/visit/clarence-house

Eltham Palace
www.english-heritage.org.uk

Jewel Tower, Westminster
www.english-heritage.org.uk

Kensington Gardens
www.royalparks.org.uk

Kensington Palace
www.hrp.org.uk/kensington-palace

Kew Palace
www.hrp.org.uk/kew-palace

Palace of Westminster
www.parliament.uk

The Queen's House, Greenwich
www.rmg.co.uk/queens-house

Royal Botanic Gardens, Kew
www.kew.org

The Royal Mews
www.rct.uk/visit/royalmews

St Paul's Cathedral
www.stpauls.co.uk

Tower of London
www.hrp.org.uk/tower-of-london

Westminster Abbey
www.westminster-abbey.org

ENGLAND

Berkhamsted Castle, Hertfordshire
www.english-heritage.org.uk

Carisbrooke Castle, Isle of Wight
www.english-heritage.org.uk

Hampton Court Palace, Surrey
www.hrp.org.uk/hampton-court-palace

Hatfield House, Hertfordshire
www.hatfield-house.co.uk

Highgrove Gardens, Gloucestershire
www.highgrovegardens.com

Leeds Castle, Kent
www.leeds-castle.com

Osborne House, Isle of Wight
www.english-heritage.org.uk

Royal Pavilion, East Sussex
brightonmuseums.org.uk

Sandringham Estate, Norfolk
www.sandringhamestate.co.uk

Walmer Castle, Kent
www.english-heritage.org.uk

Windsor Castle, Berkshire
www.rct.uk/visit/windsorcastle

SCOTLAND

Balmoral (grounds and gardens), Aberdeenshire
www.balmoralcastle.com

Edinburgh Castle
www.edinburghcastle.scot

Falkland Palace and Garden, Fife
www.nts.org.uk

Glamis Castle, Angus
www.glamis-castle.co.uk

Linlithgow Palace, West Lothian
www.historicenvironment.scot

Palace of Holyroodhouse, Edinburgh
www.rct.uk/visit/palace-of-holyroodhouse

Stirling Castle, Stirling
www.stirlingcastle.scot

WALES

Caernarfon Castle, Gwynedd
www.caernarfon-castle.co.uk

NORTHERN IRELAND

Hillsborough Castle, County Down
www.hrp.org.uk/hillsborough-castle